HUMPTY TRUMPTY

ISBN-10 1984332961
ISBN-13 978- 1984332967

"I WILL BUILD A GREAT, GREAT WALL
ON OUR SOUTHERN BORDER,
AND I WILL MAKE MEXICO PAY FOR THE WALL,
MARK MY WORDS."

—DONALD TRUMP